MY CHRISTIAN ABC COLORING BOOK

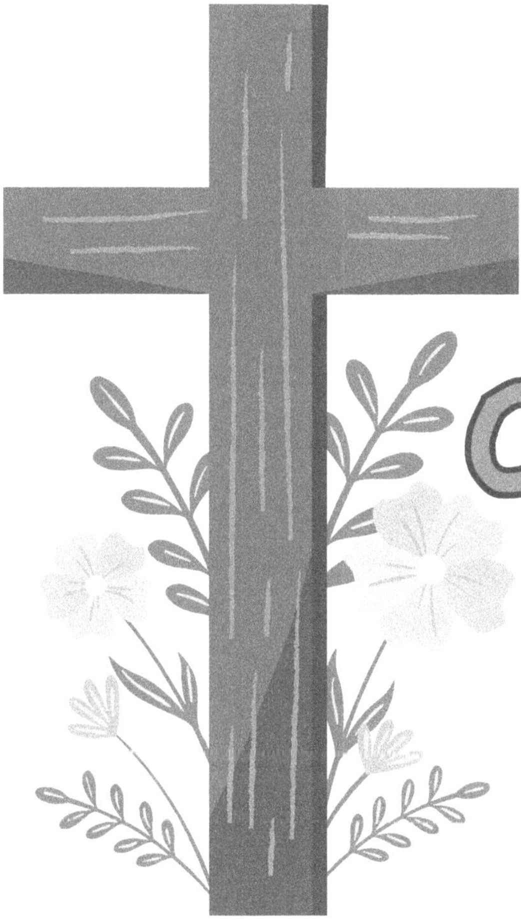

Name: ______________________

Age: ______________________

Jesus said to him, "I am the way, and the truth, and the life. No one comes to the Father except through me." - John 14:6 (ESV)

Aa

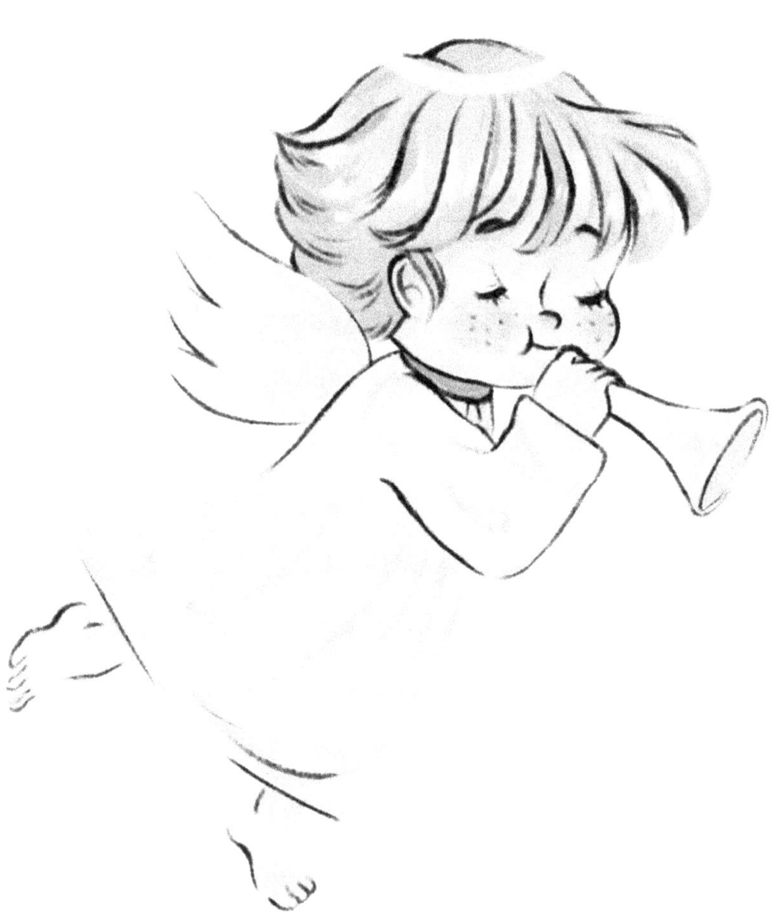

Angel

Bb

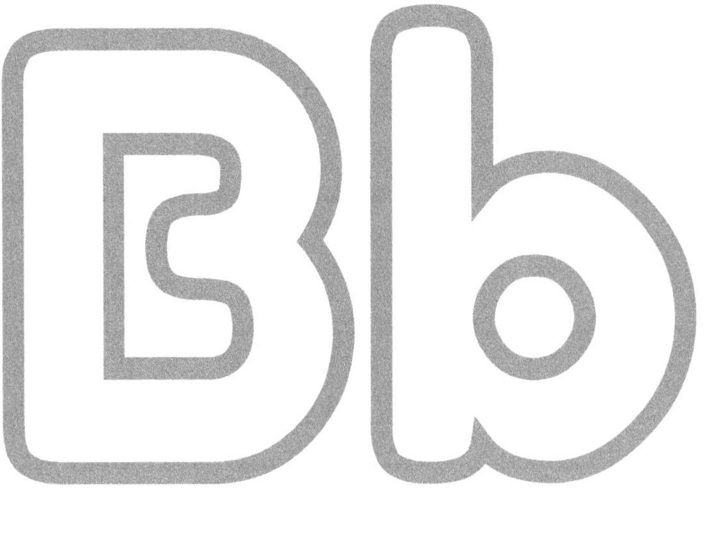

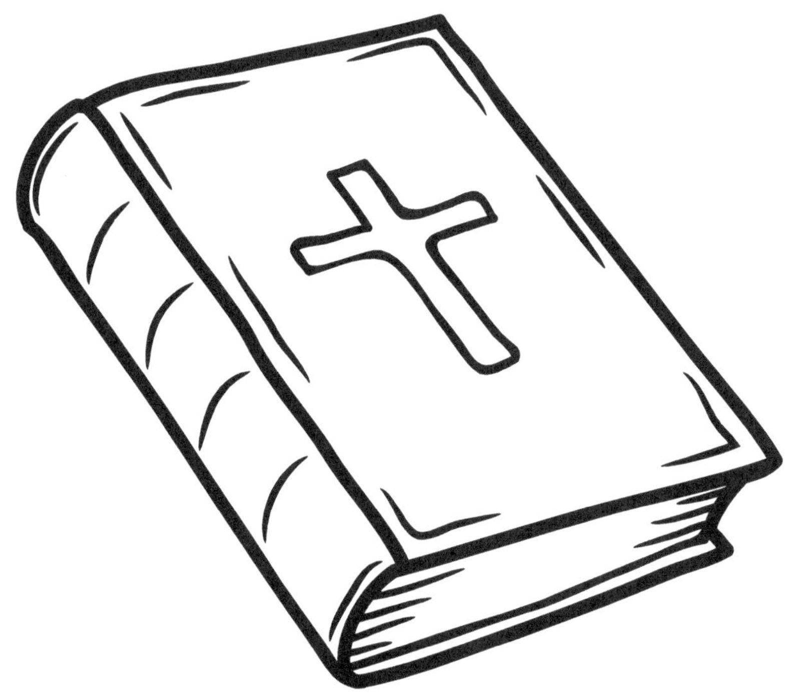

Bible

Cc

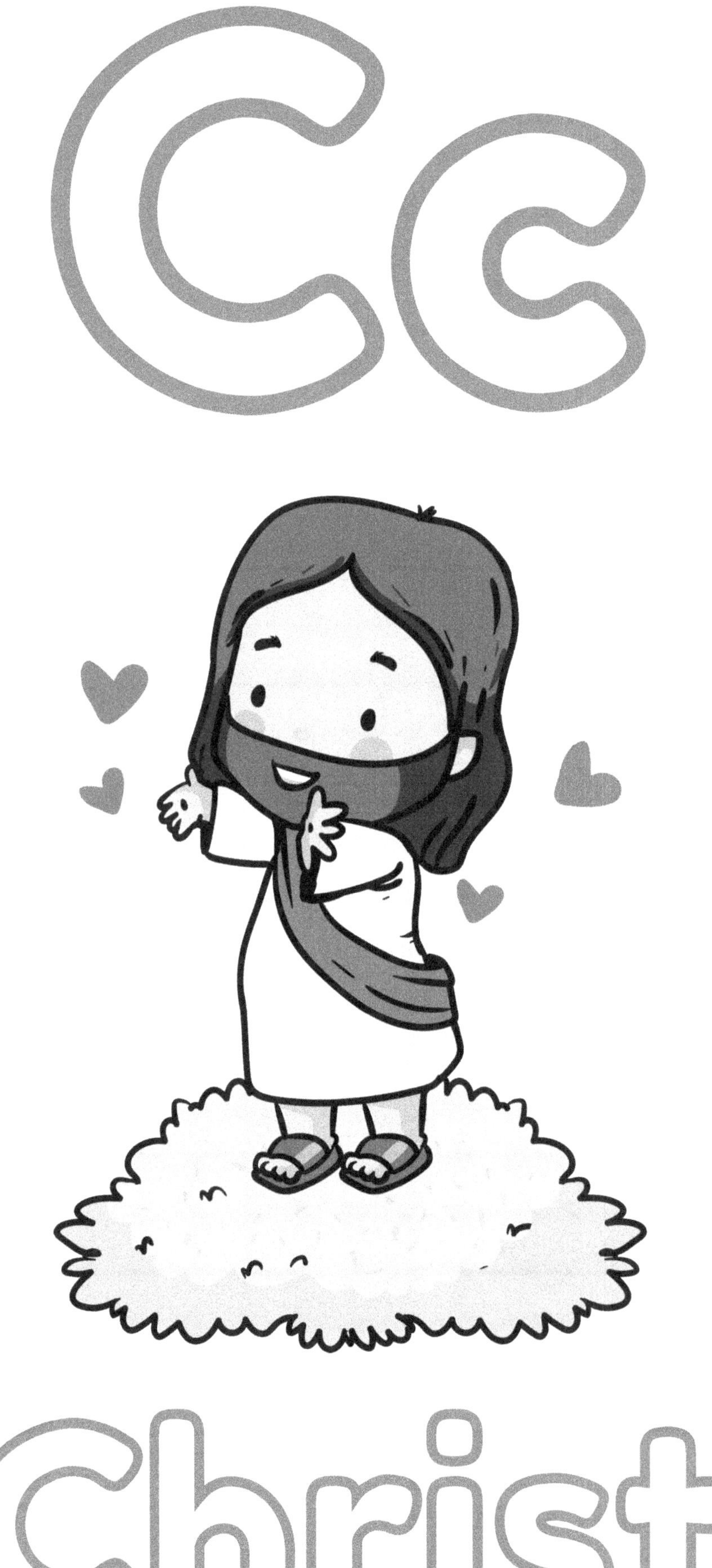

Christ

Dd

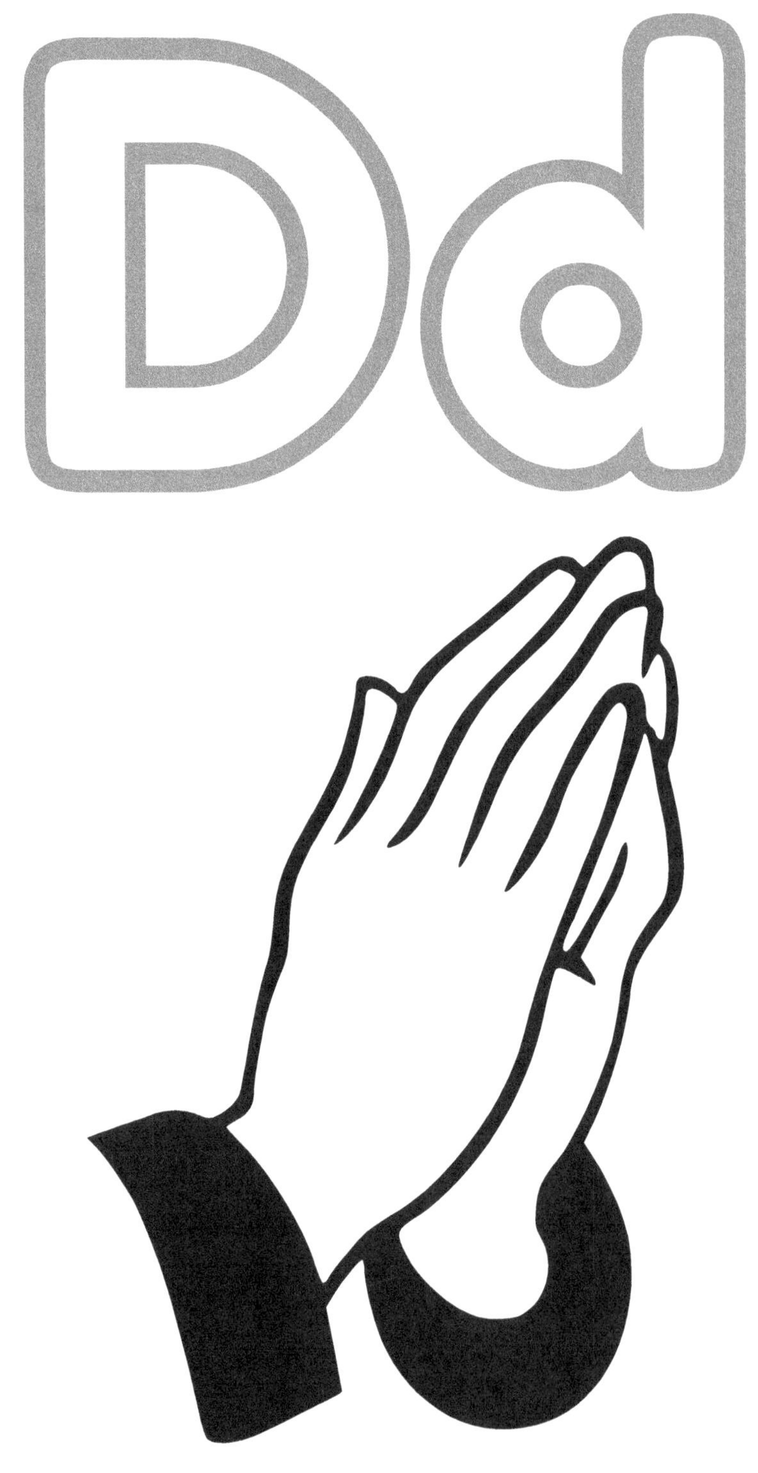

Devoted

E e

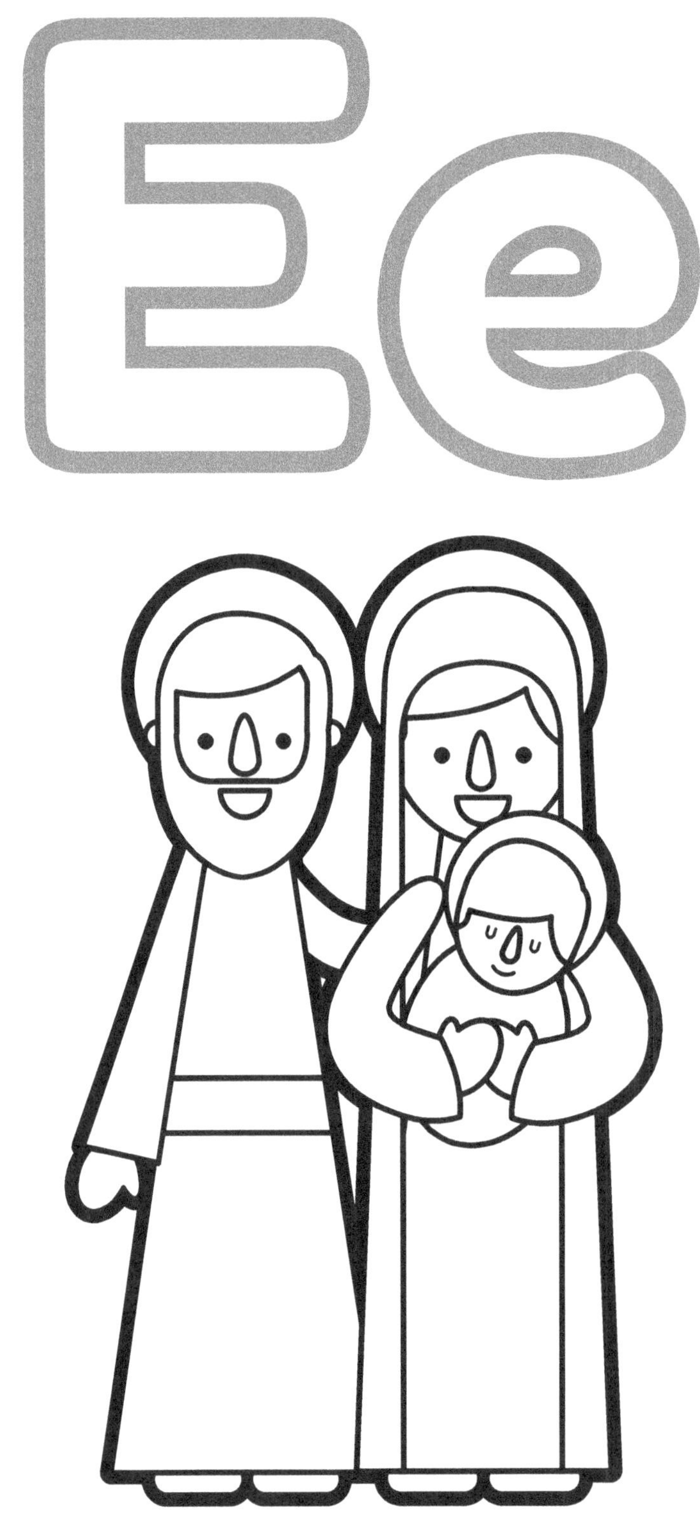

Emmanuel

Ff

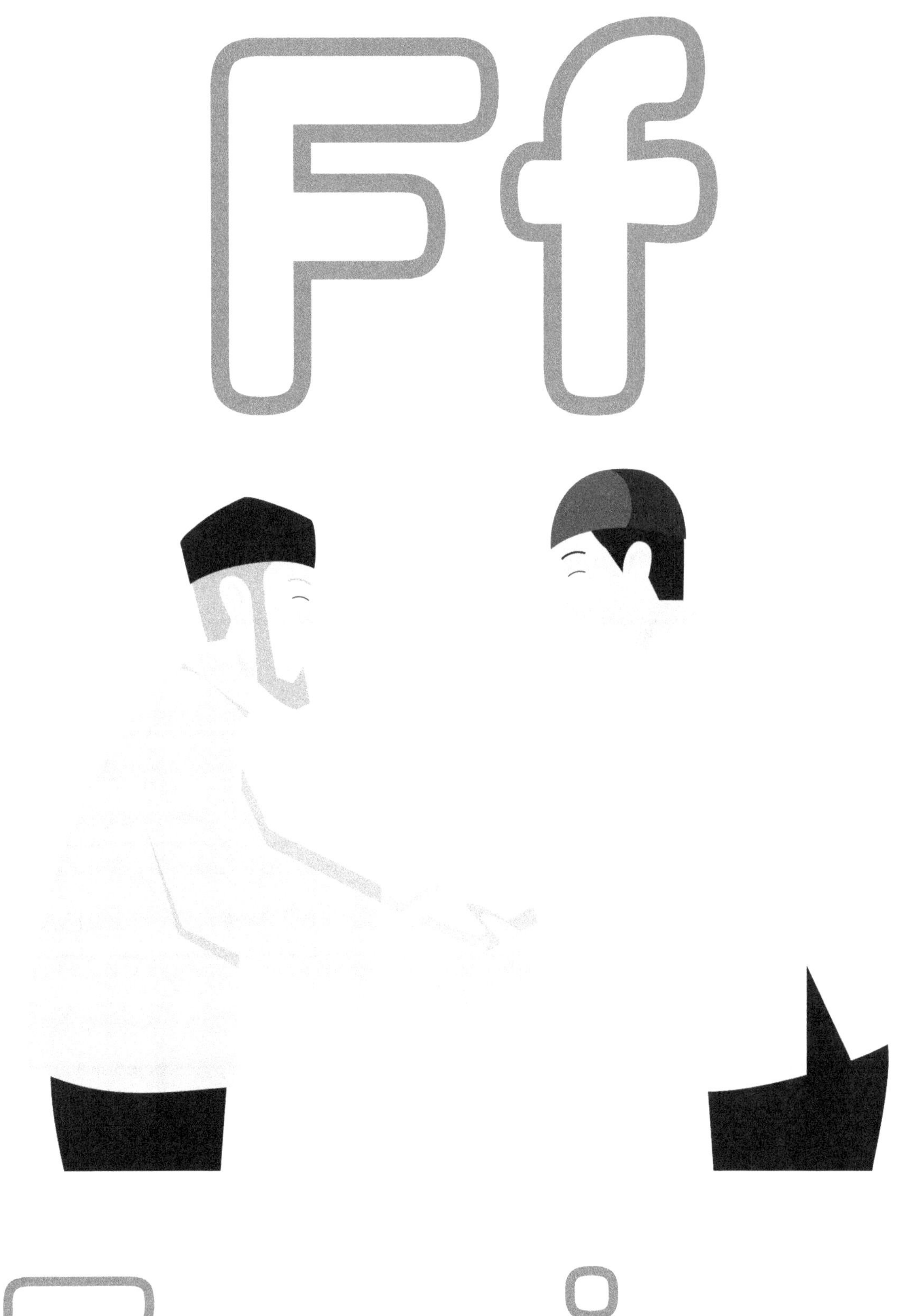

Forgive

Gg

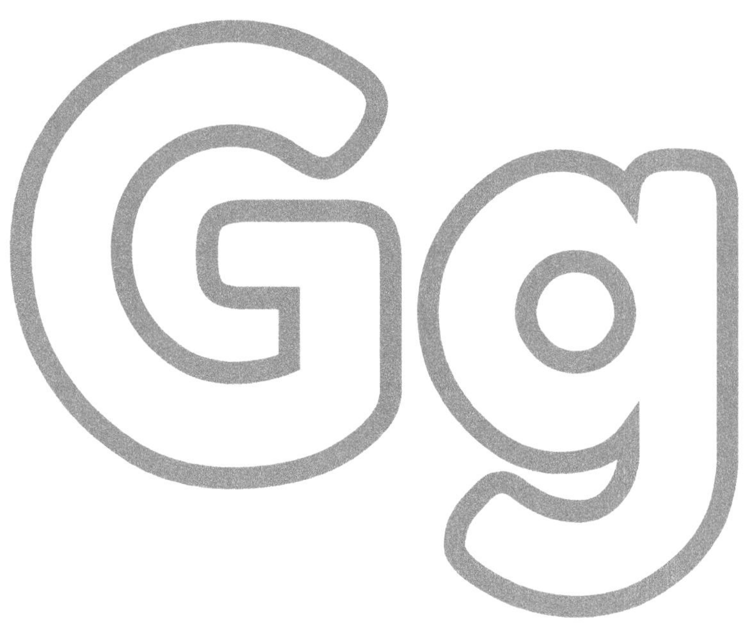

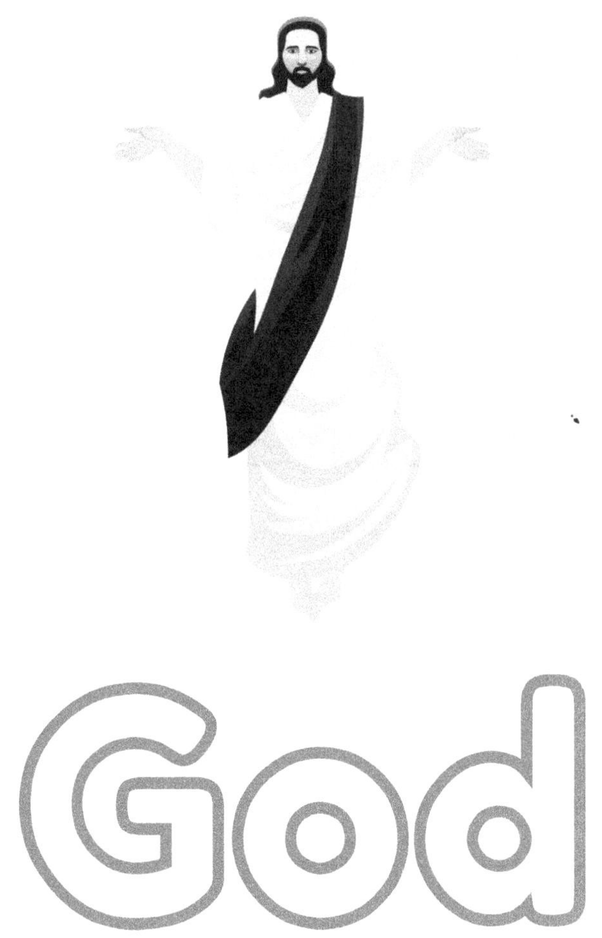

God

Hh

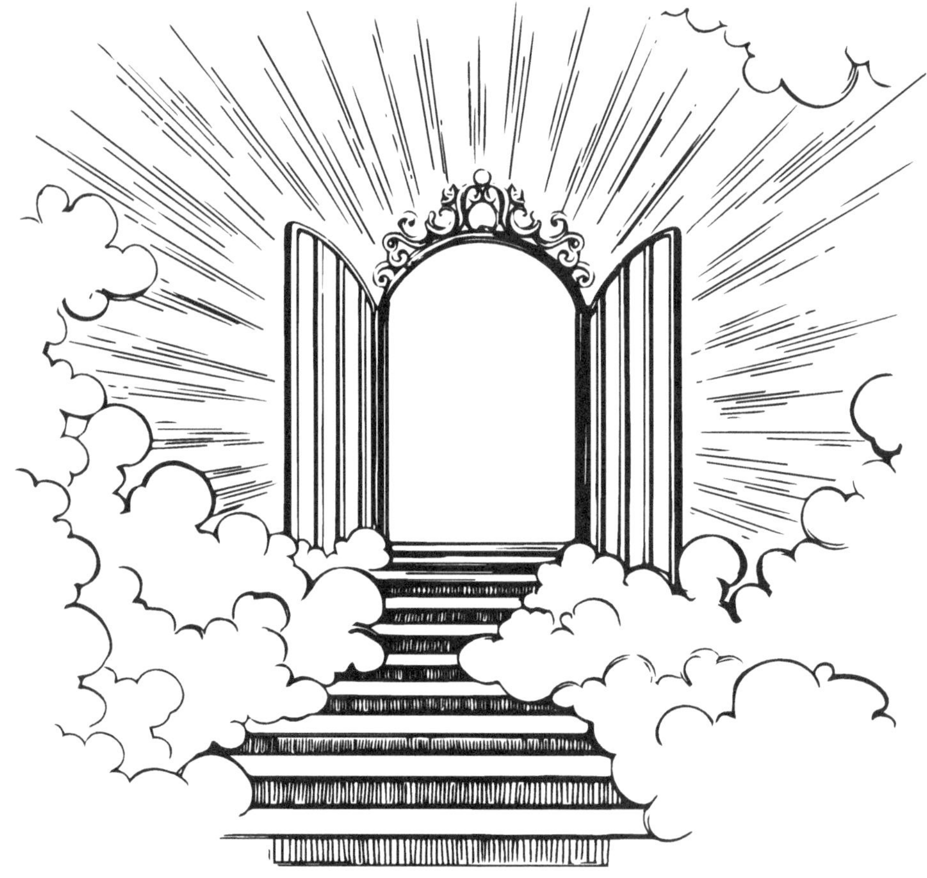

Heaven

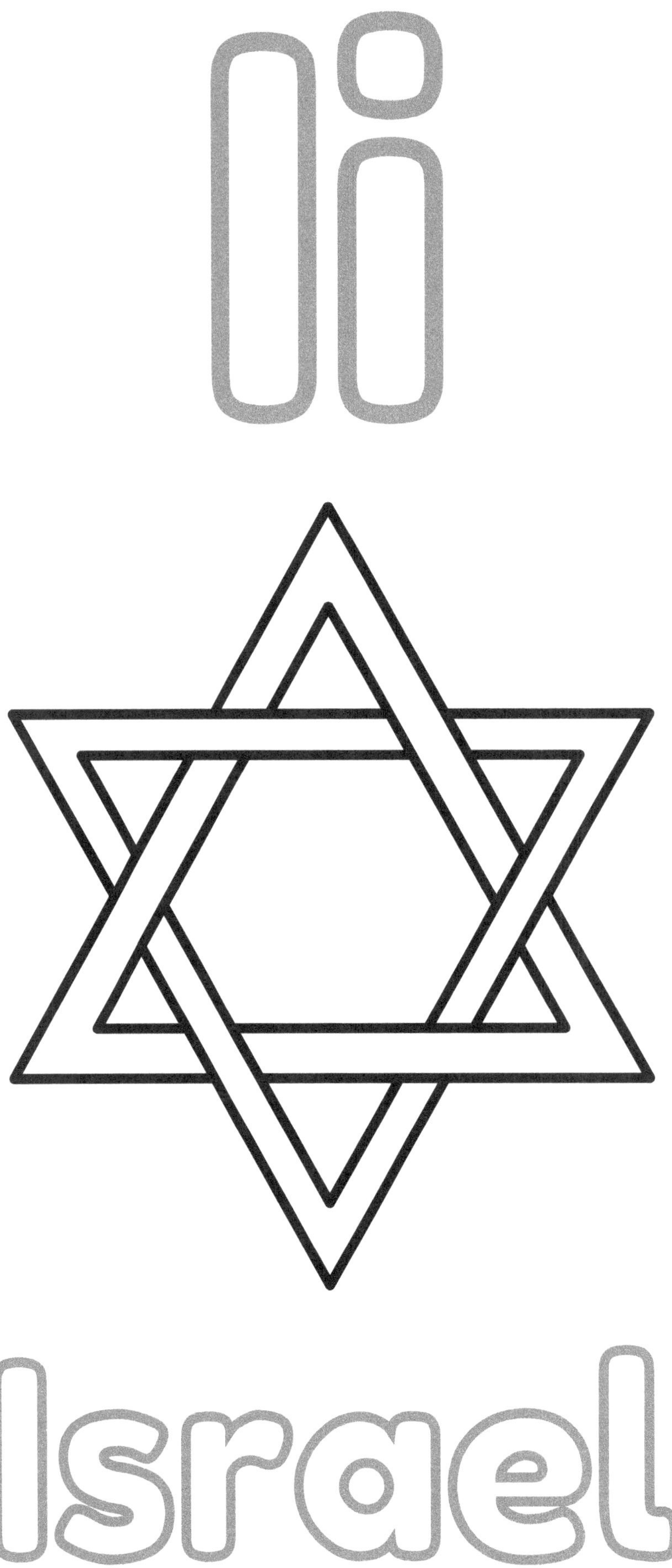

Ii
Israel

Jj

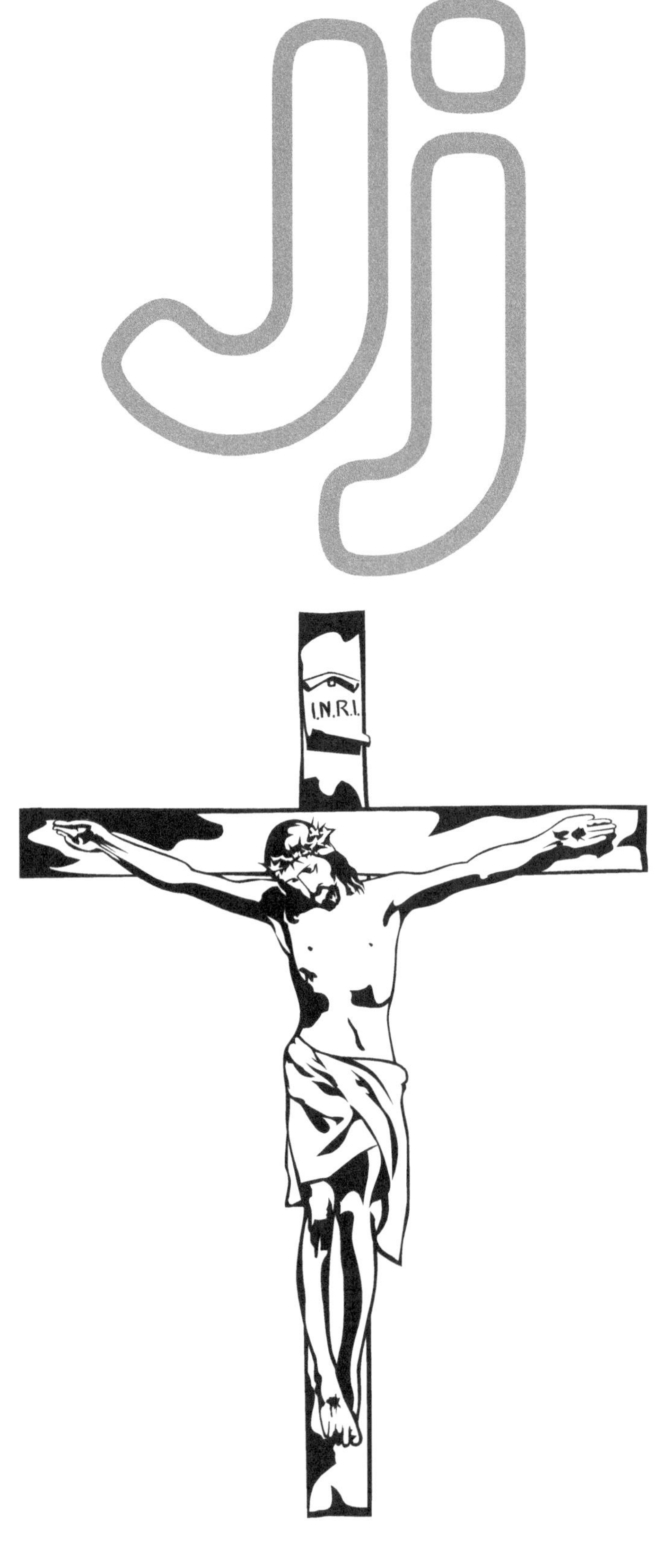

Jesus

Kk

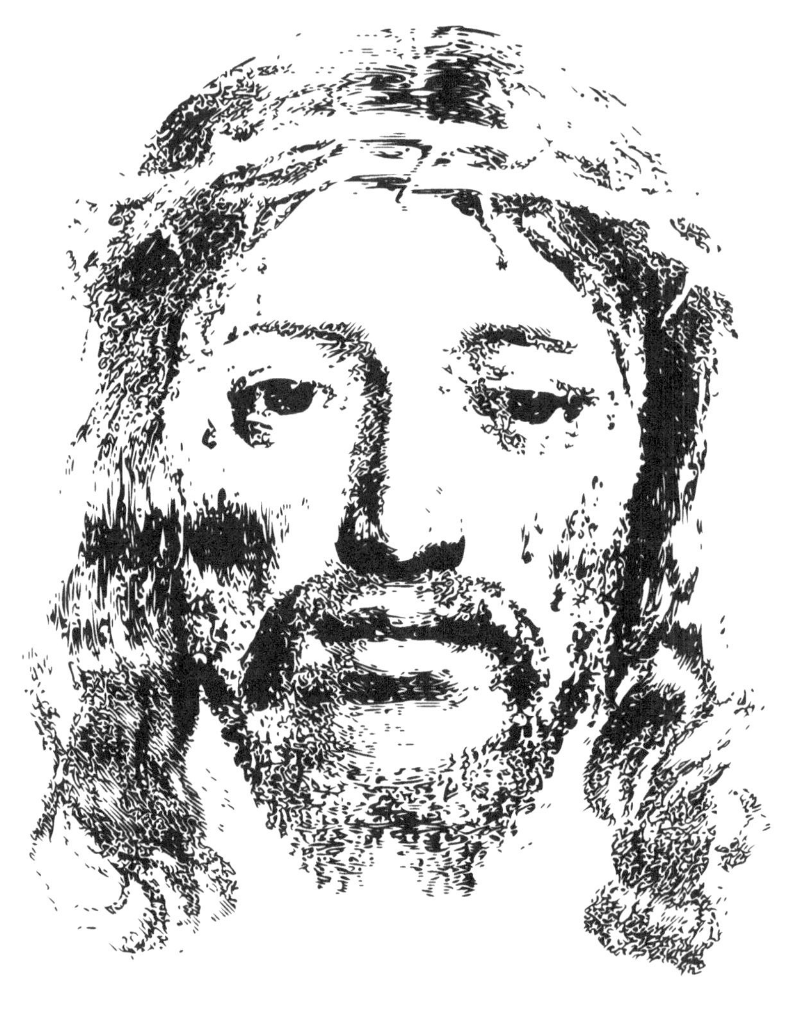

King

Ll

Love

Mm

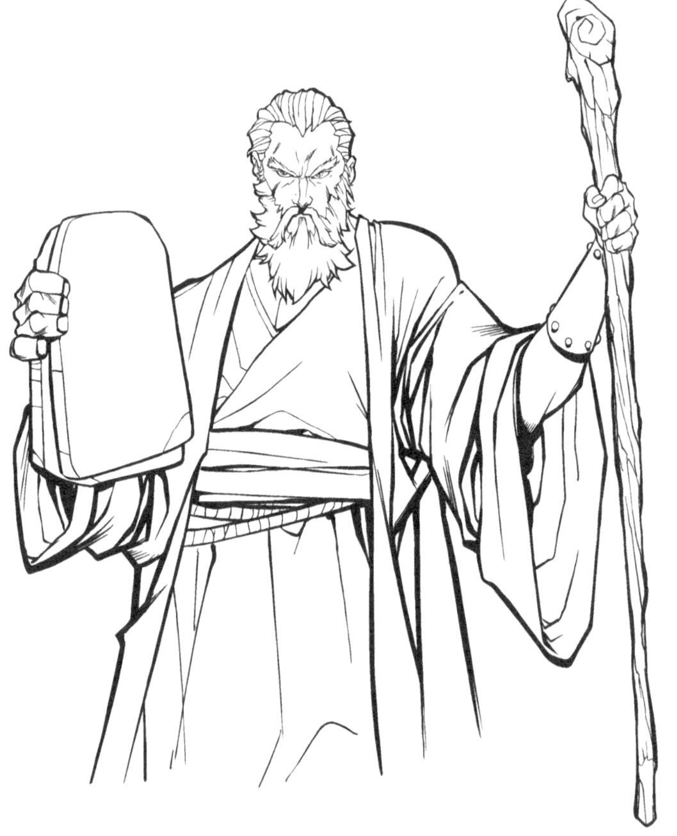

Moses

Nn

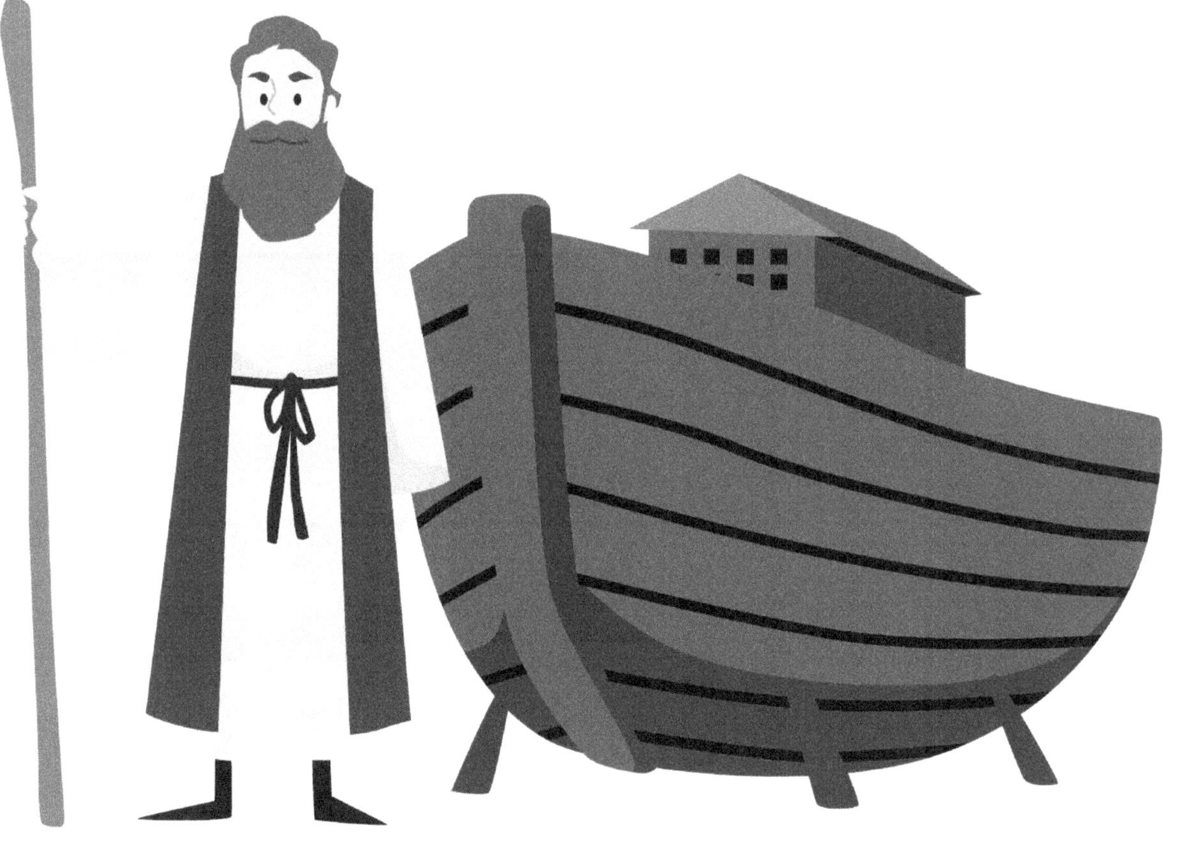

Noah

Oo

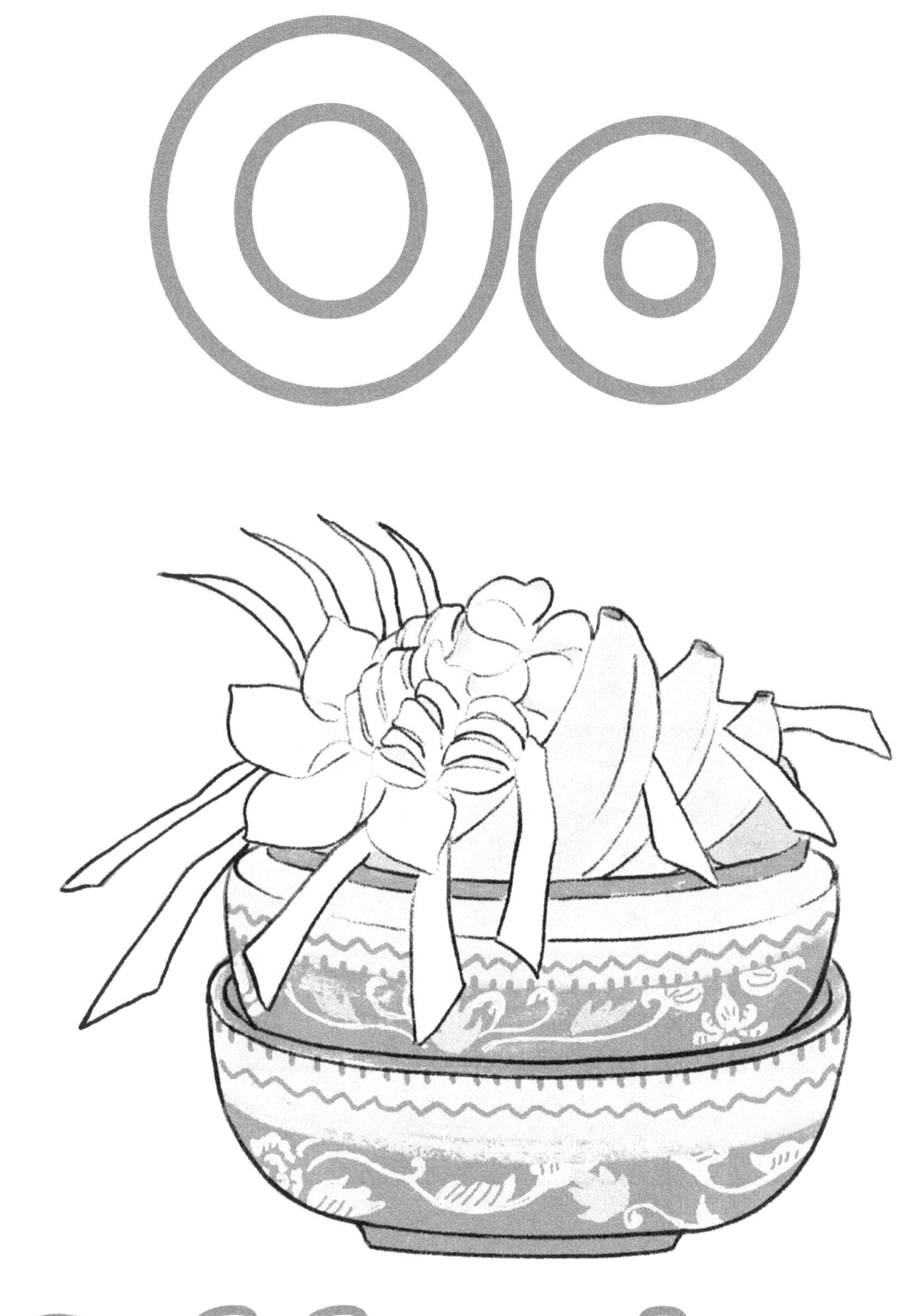

Offering

Pp

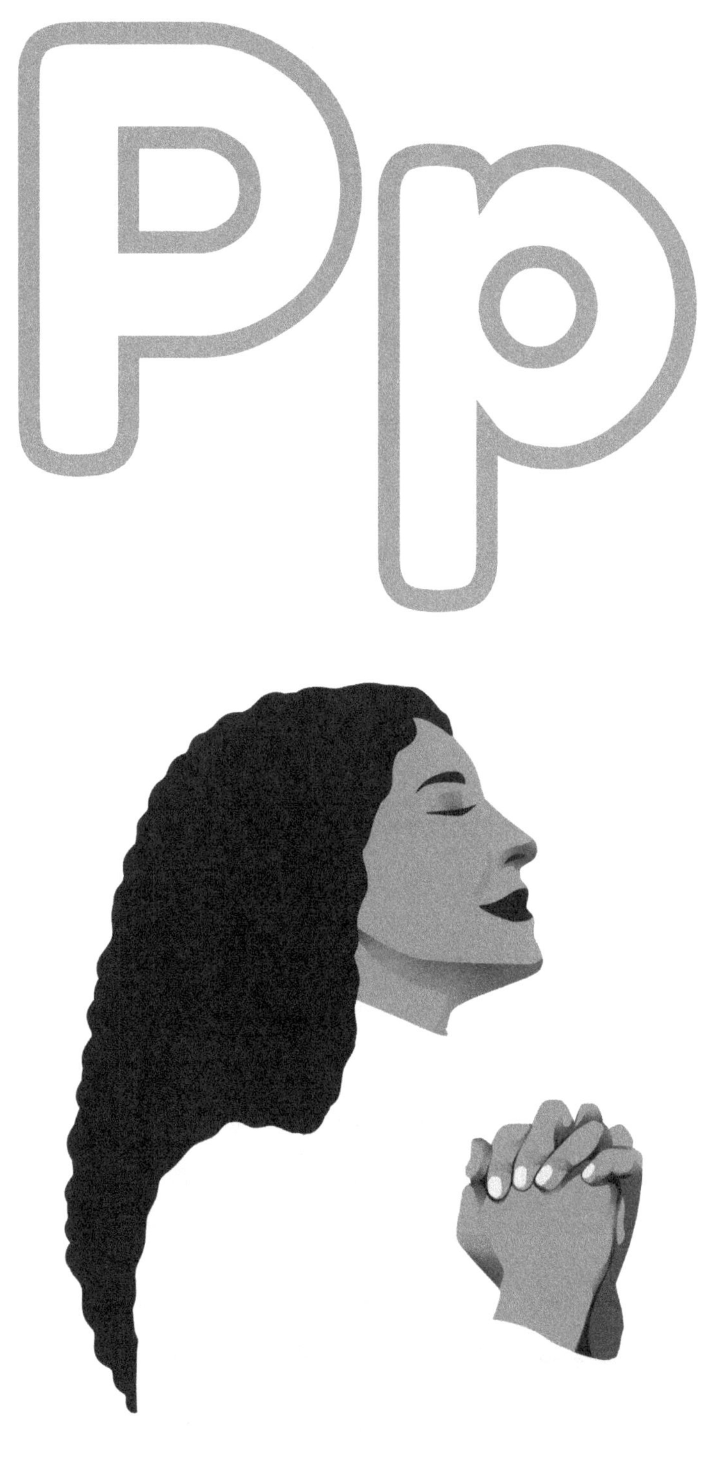

Pray

Qq

Queen

Esther

Rr

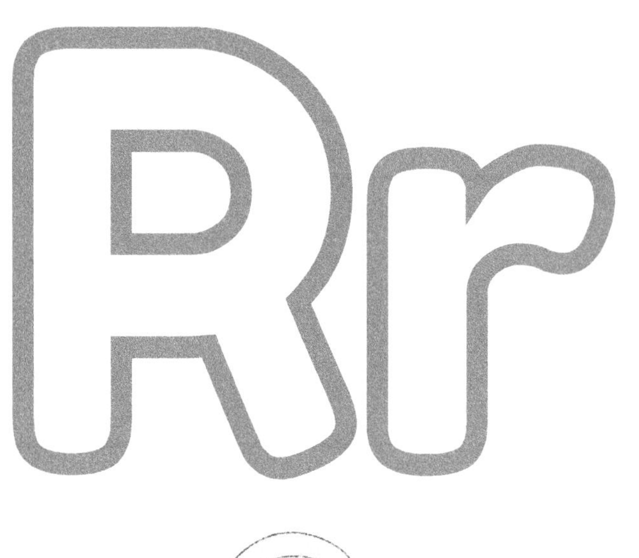

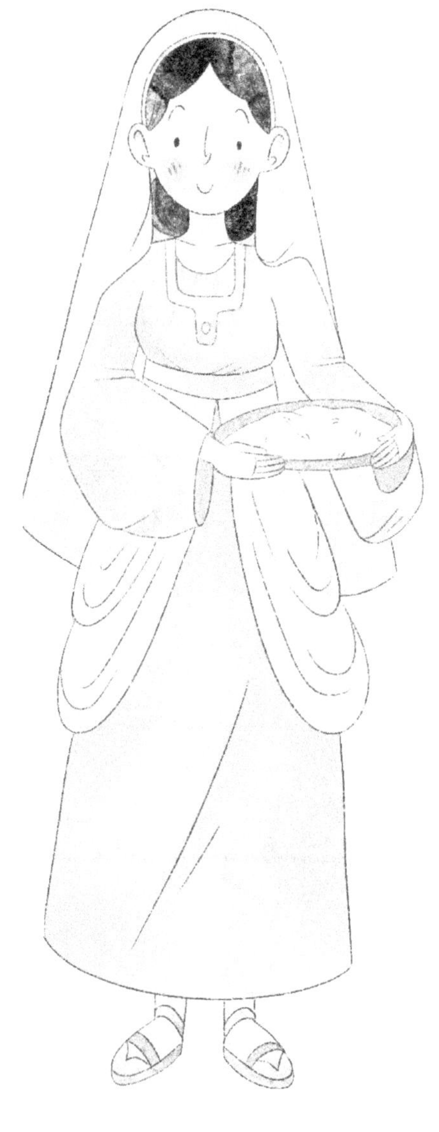

Ruth

Ss

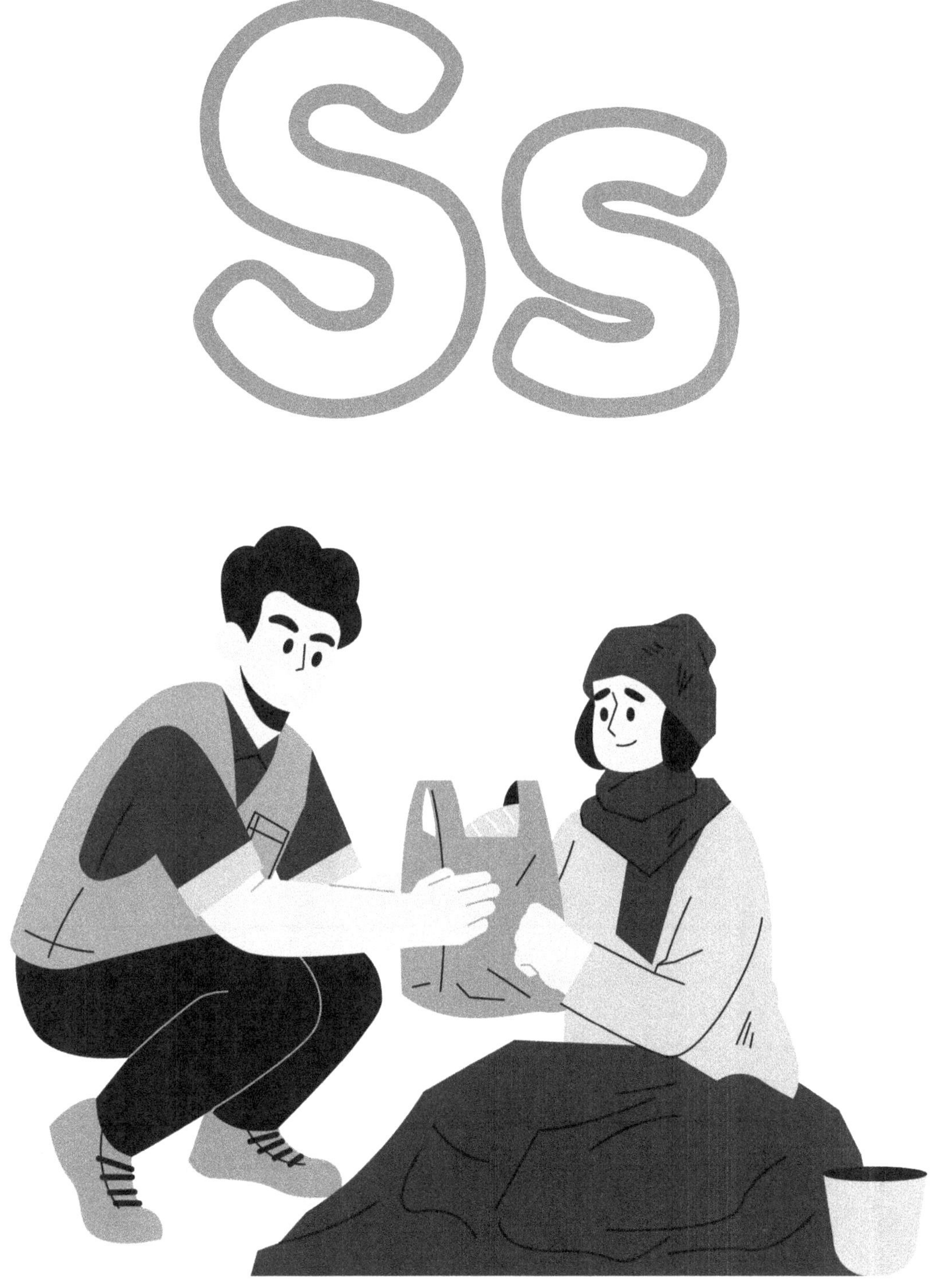

Sacrifice

Tt

Trinity

Uu

BE UNIQUE

Unique

Vv

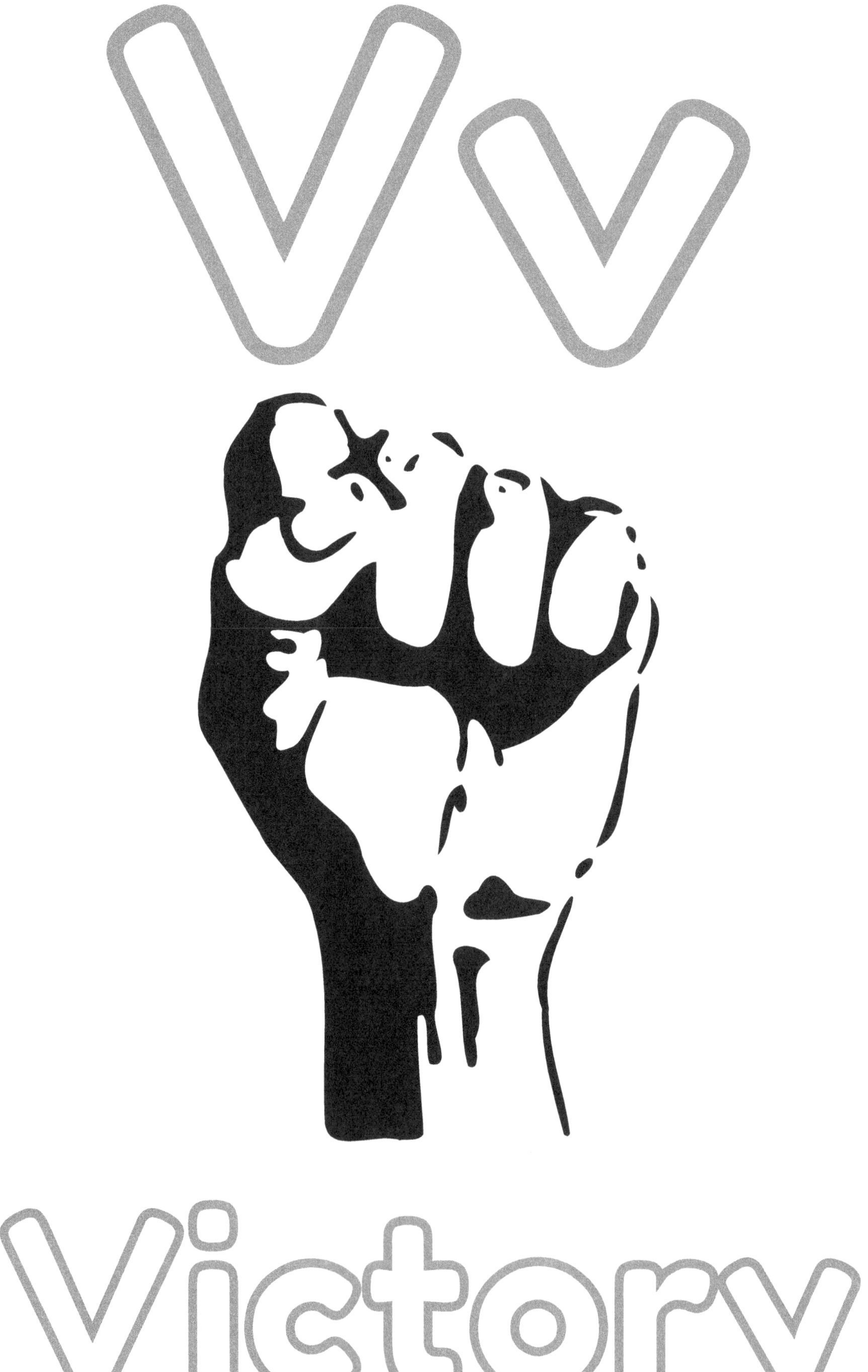

Victory

Ww

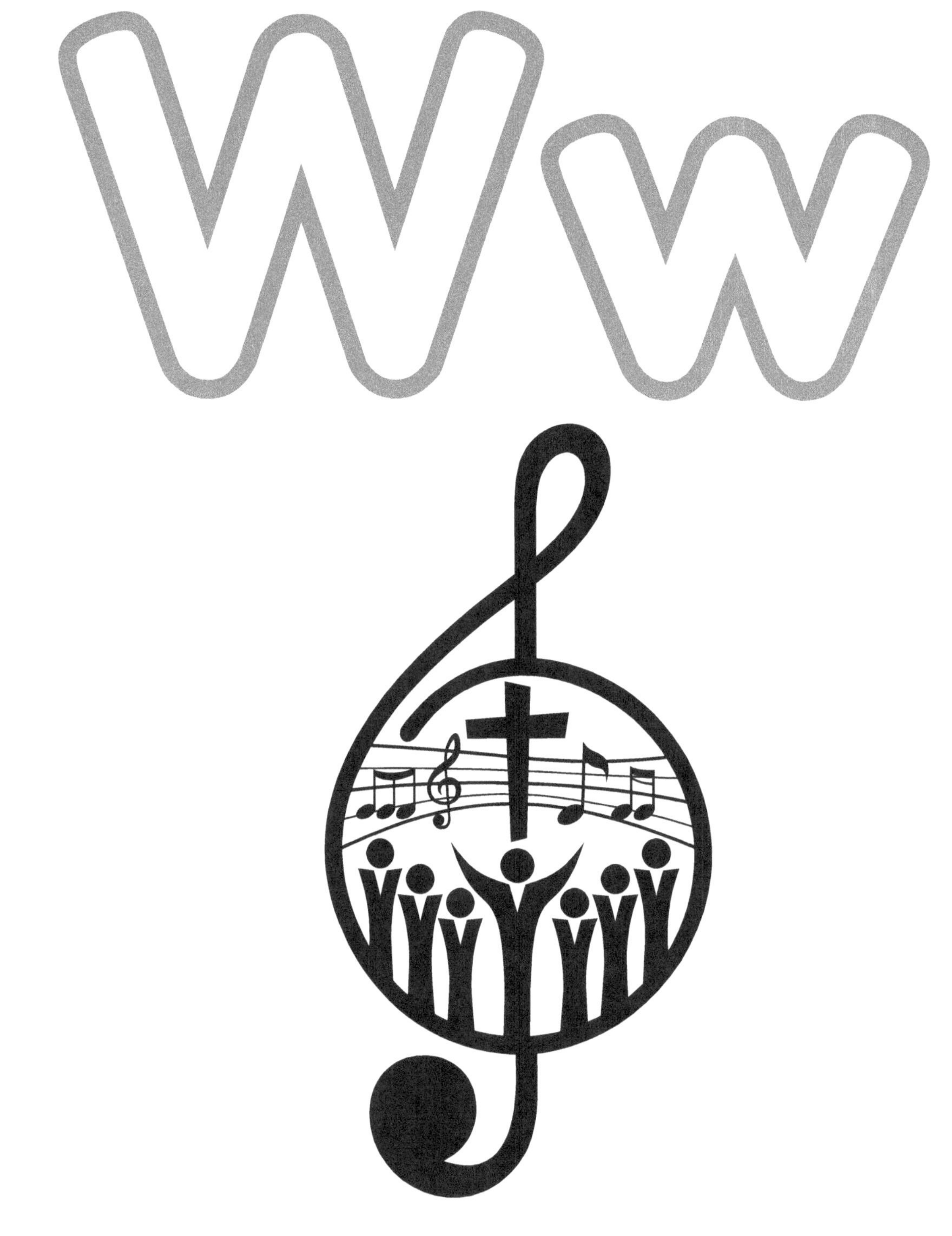

Worship

Xx

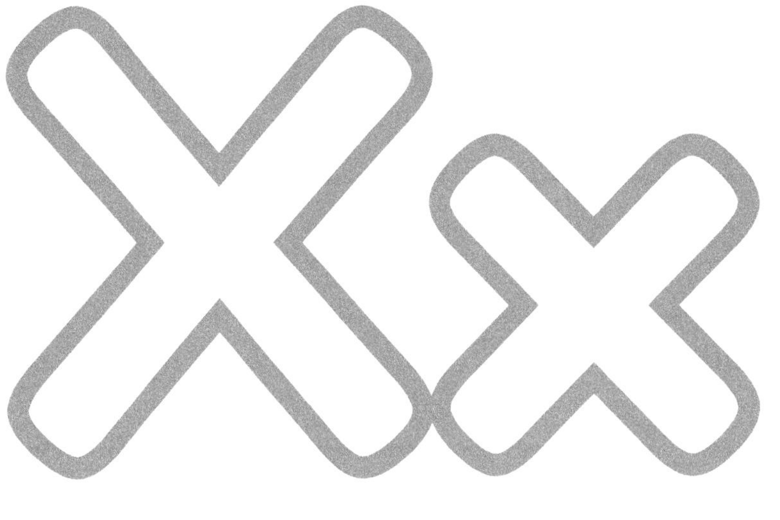

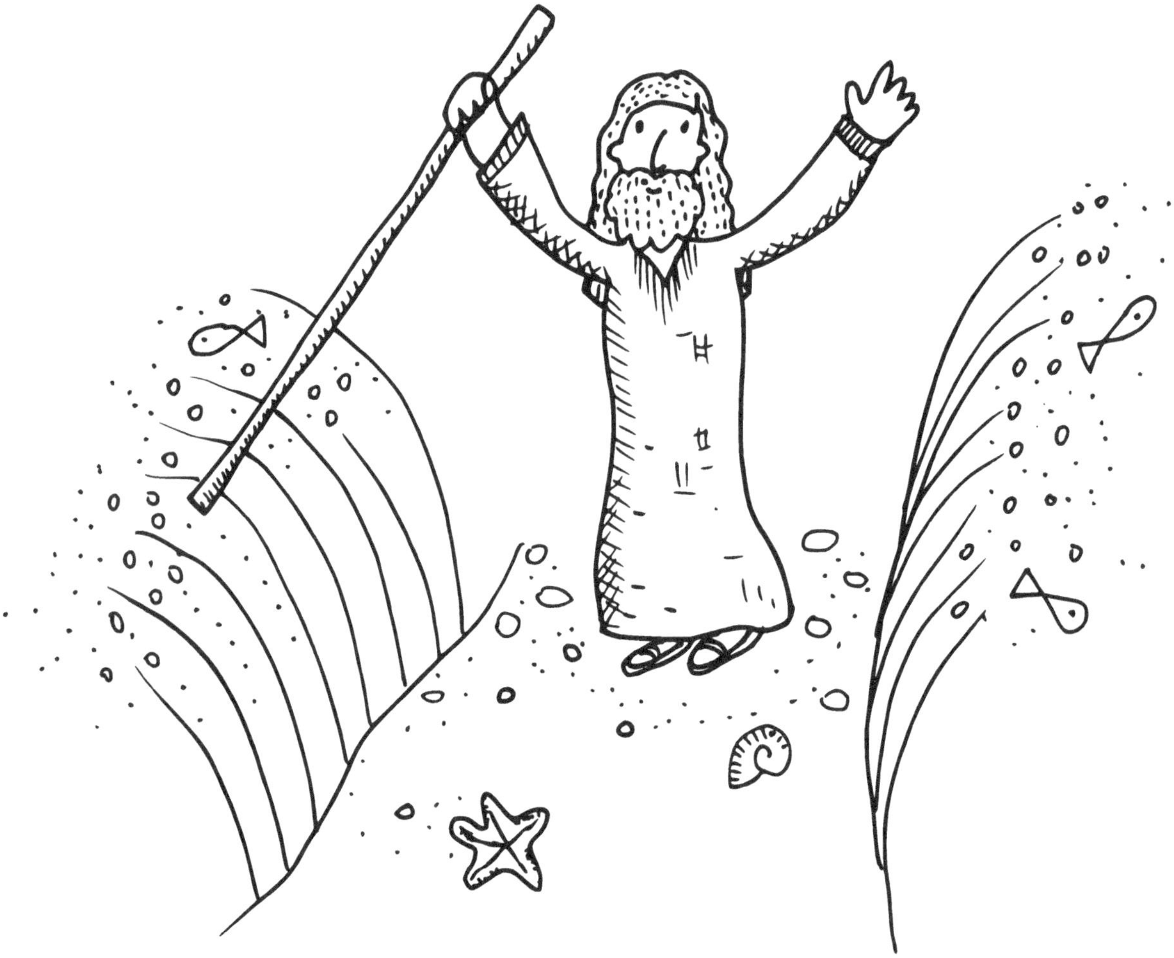

eXodus

Y y

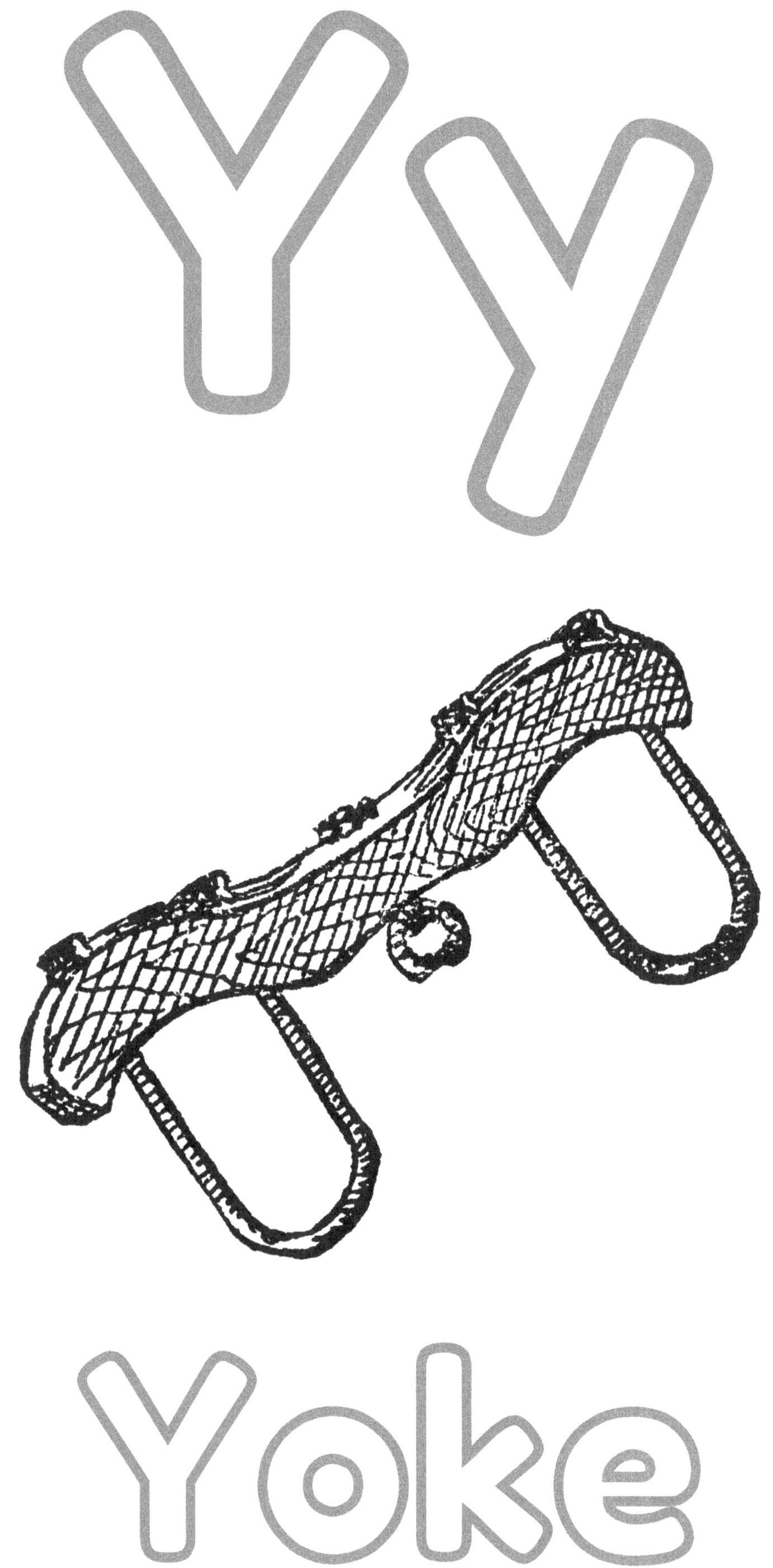

Yoke

Zz

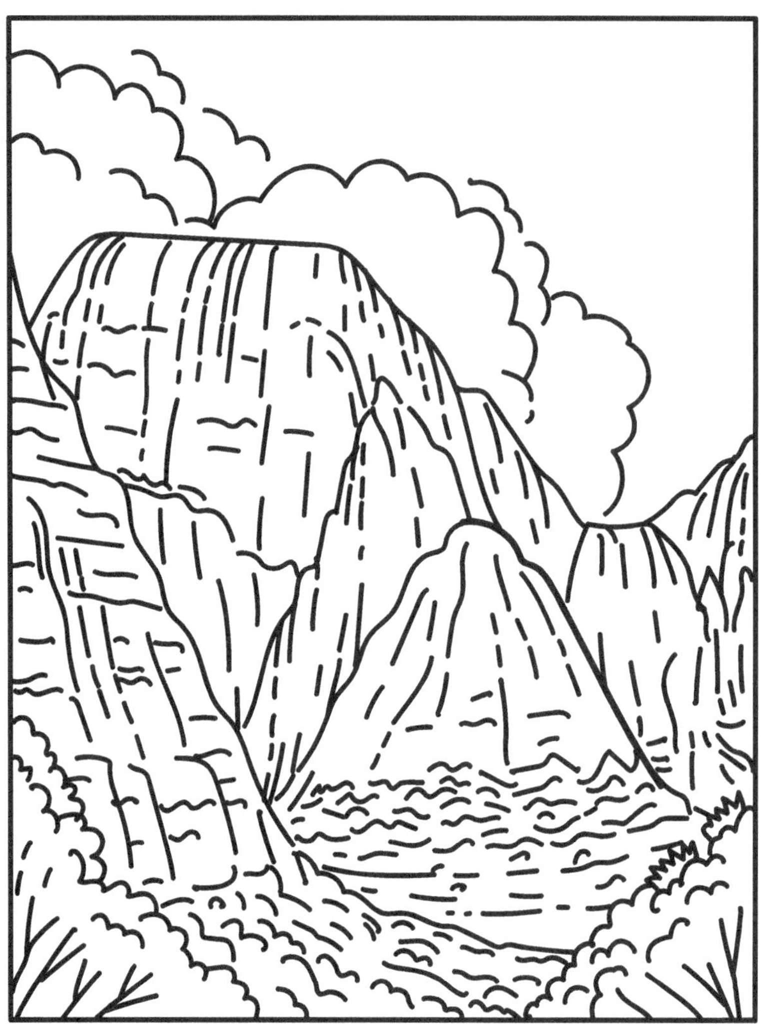

Zion